HOW WE USED TO LIVE

1936-1953

FREDA KELSALL

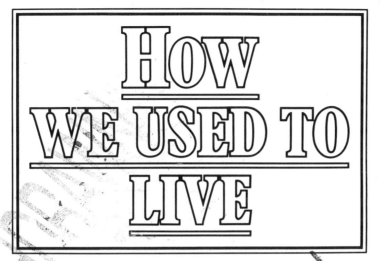

£8 95

Macdonald **by arrangement with Yorkshire Television**

Contents

Acknowledgements

We wish to thank the following organisations and individuals for their assistance, and for making available material in their collections.

B.B.C. Copyright Photograph, 26(R)
B.B.C. Hulton Picture Library, 4, 8(B), 9(BL),(BR), 11(B), 12(T), 17(TR),(BL), 25(B), 29(B), 35(B), 36(B), 37(TL),(BL), 41(B), 45(T),(B)
B.P.C. Library, 7(TL),(TR), 11(TL),(TR), 16(L),(R), 17(BR), 18(R), 20(T), 23(B), 26(L), 27(BR), 30, 31(TR), 35(TL), 38(T), 40(T), 43(TR),(BR)
Barnaby's Picture Library, 5(TR),(BL), 14(R), 21(TR),(BR), 28(T)
Conservative Research Department, 6
Fox Photos, 14(L), 19(BL)
John Frost Historical Newspaper Service, 7(TL), 11(TL),(TR)
General Electric Company, 43(BR)
Dennis Gifford, 7(TR), 16(R), 18(R), 20(T), 26(L), 27(BR), 30, 38(T), 43(TR)
Tim Healey Collection, 10(T), 21(BL), 25(T), 29(TL),(TR), 33(TL), 33(BL), 35(T),(C), 37(TR), 46
Imperial War Museum, 13(BR), 15(TL),(TR),(BL), 16(L), 17(BR), 19(TR),(BR), 22(R), 23(B), 34(L),(R), 40(T), 44(T)
The Kent Messenger, 21(TL), 24–25
London Express Features, 13(CL), 33(BL), 35(C)
Museum of London, 12(B)
Peter Myers, 46
Popperfoto, 15(BR), 20(B), 23(T), 24, 42, 43(BL), 47
Punch, 17(TL)
The Rank Organization Limited, 27(T)

John Topham Picture Library, 7(B), 8(T), 9(T), 10(B), 13(BL), 19(TL), 27(BL), 28(B), 29(C), 32, 33(TR),(BR), 36(T), 38(B), 40(B), 41(T), 43(TL), 44(B)
Weidenfeld and Nicolson (*Keep Smiling Through*), 12(B), 13(T),(CL),(BR), 15(BR), 17(TL), 19(BL), 21(TL), 22(L), 24–25, 27(T), 31(TL), 44(T)
Yorkshire Television, 3, 5(TL)

Cover pictures

Wartime rationing (B.B.C. Hulton Picture Library); *The jitterbugging craze* (John Topham Picture Library); *Listening to the wireless* (T.B.W.A.); *Stamps from the reigns of George VI and Elizabeth II* (Tim Healey Collection); Back cover: *Holiday-time, 1936* (Barnaby's Picture Library)

Artists
Peter Acty, 39
Hayward Art Group, 30–31, 47

A Macdonald Book

First published 1981
Reprinted 1983, 1985
Macdonald & Co. (Publishers) Ltd
Maxwell House
Worship Street
London EC2A 2EN
A member of BPCC plc

©Macdonald & Co.
(Publishers) Ltd 1981

ISBN 0 356 06298 8 (cased)
ISBN 0 356 06299 6 (limp)

Printed and bound by
Henri Proost, Turnhout, Belgium

Historical adviser: Norman Longmate
Editor: Tim Healey
In-house editor: Lis Edwards
Production: Philip Hughes
Picture research: Georgina Barker

Introduction

In the new suburbs built between the wars in Britain, a man in a secure job could hope to raise a well-spaced family in modest comfort. Families could save up for occasional treats and luxuries, a holiday even, and there was the garden to enjoy, the wireless, and local opportunities for sport and recreation. If they kept in good health and on friendly terms with the neighbours life would be easy.

For the Government, keeping on friendly terms with the neighbours was not so simple. There were forces at work which, while promising an end to poverty and unemployment, held sinister menace. In Britain few were in favour of revolutionary Communism and few joined fascist rallies; many more admitted that there were social inequalities, but believed that these would be redressed eventually.

When it became clear that battle must be joined to check the power of aggressive dictatorships, Britain put aside suburban comfort for six traumatic years of war. The war effort meant loss of sleep as well as loss of life. There was spectacular heroism alongside the more mundane disturbance of being uprooted, queuing, going short of everyday items, and housing strangers. Many learnt the grief and terror of not knowing the whereabouts of their nearest and dearest. The war meant being controlled as never before, and it meant being united as never before.

Victory and the unity of purpose which brought it about yielded an electorate which was unwilling to return to the old social order. The country turned to new leaders to tackle post-war recovery and the national debt. There followed six more years of hard economic struggle before the suburban home-buyers of the thirties could begin to relax and enjoy the comforts they had sought some fifteen years previously.

▲ The new Yorkshire Television series of *How We Used to Live* embraces events during the reign of King George VI as they affected the family of Arthur Hodgkins, a railwayman living in a fictitious Yorkshire town. The story begins with the abdication of Edward VIII and includes the dramatic changes of World War Two. It ends with the coronation of Queen Elizabeth II. In the years between, Arthur and his wife Mabel, together with their four children, experience something of the way of life described in this book.

Home Comforts

In the mid-thirties, Britain was still recovering from economic depression. Nevertheless, light industries prospered, especially those concerned with building and equipping homes. Convenient transport by road and rail meant that the family wage-earner did not have to live near the job. Suburban housing estates were built close to railway stations, and factories sprang up in 'ribbon developments' along main roads. By 1935 laws were needed to curb this unplanned building. London's rapid expansion was checked by preserving a Green Belt of countryside around it.

Electricity became available in most homes after the National Grid was completed in 1933 at a cost of £27 million. Sales of electrical goods rose. Mains water and drainage were taken for granted, and most towns had a local gas works. Motor car manufacture was thriving, and many new houses were built with garages.

People in secure employment could buy their homes with a mortgage instead of paying almost as much each week in rent. A £5 deposit followed by weekly payments of 12/6 (62½p), secured a two-storey 'semi' with three bedrooms. Typical family homes valued at £500 near London might cost only £400 in the provinces.

Houses were often decorated inside in pale distemper, with narrow, patterned friezes along the walls under the picture rails. Ornaments and pictures were kept to a minimum and furnishings were in geometric shapes.

Metal window frames allowed houses to be designed with big windows, adding to the feeling of light and space compared to homes in the old, cramped urban terraces. Even better, some of the green fields on which these houses were built were preserved as gardens so children no longer had to play in the streets. Gardening and gardening shops flourished.

▼King George VI and Queen Elizabeth with their daughters Elizabeth (born 1926) and Margaret Rose outside the miniature house given to the two princesses by the people of Wales. As Duke and Duchess of York, the couple were known to prefer a quiet family life as a contrast to Royal engagements. Before the abdication of Edward VIII the family had been settled at the Royal Lodge in Windsor Great Park with their pets (particularly corgis) for company and a garden to develop, interests shared by many people in Britain's suburbs.

▲ This house, used by Yorkshire Television for the series, is typical of the suburban 'semis' of the thirties. They often included features such as diamond-shaped leaded glass in windows and the 'sunrise' theme on doors and gates. The motif of the rising sun was echoed on many products of the time.

▶ A middle-class man in work could afford to buy his comfortable home, often for less than the unemployed man paid in rent. Income tax was increased by 3d. or 6d. (2½p) in the pound during the mid-thirties for extra defence spending. A married man with two children paid £1.13.4d (£1.67) tax a year on an annual income of £400 in 1937.

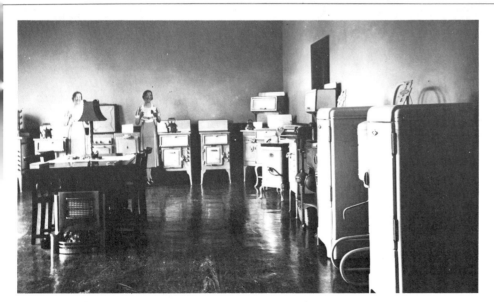

Electricity in the Home

◀ The Appliance Room at Electric House in London shows a range of cookers, washing machines, fires and refrigerators. These novel electrical goods helped to simplify housework and overcome the 'problem' for middle-class families of doing without servants. Table lamps and standard lamps graced many homes; suction cleaners and electric irons were popular; electric fires were clean, and saved carrying coal. Women debated the relative merits of gas and electric cookers. But few had gone in for electric power to speed the family wash and there were very few domestic refrigerators in Britain in 1938.

Domestic Budgets

Before World War Two, the average income was under £3 per week. A bus driver brought home £2.15/- (£2.75). For the unemployed there was the Means Test which allowed a married man 24/- (£1.20) for himself and his wife. The father was often the only breadwinner but it was possible to feed a family of five on half his wages. There were fewer working mothers than there are today, and no family allowances. Many women lost their job if they married. Their place was considered to be in the home, where most children returned for lunch. Often the oldest child had to leave school at fourteen and go out to work to bring in more money.

Regular weekly outgoings on essentials made it difficult to save for 'luxuries'. Between 10/- and 15/- (50–75p) could go on rent. Fuel cost at least 6/- (30p). Families setting up home could buy furniture on hire purchase. A new bedroom suite in 'figured oak' cost 9 guineas (£9.45) or 21 monthly payments of 10/- (50p).

Clothing cost about 1/- (5p) a week per person, and much clothing and furniture was bought second-hand. In the poorest areas some people lived on bread, tea and potatoes, and children suffered from malnutrition.

Smoking was not recognised as a health hazard. Black Cat and Park Drive cigarettes cost 6d. (2½p) for 15. Cadbury's Fruit and Nut chocolate was 1/- (5p) for 12 ozs. Those with money to spend on luxuries could buy a Hercules bicycle for under £4 or a wireless set from about £8. But an unemployed man could scarcely afford a daily newspaper at 1d. (½p).

▼ An election poster from the early thirties, featuring the wife and children of an unemployed man. Unemployment remained around 1½ million during the mid-thirties, but rose above the two million mark in the spring of 1939.

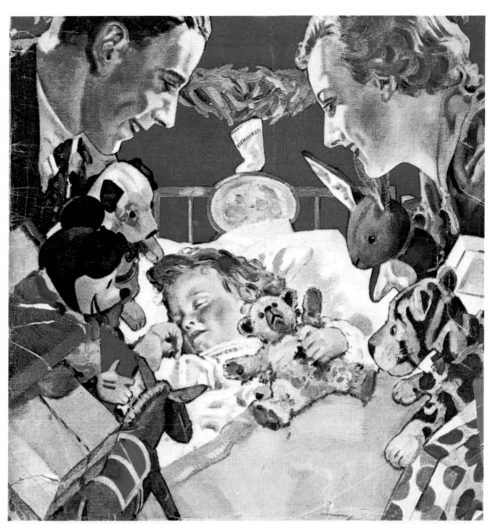

▲ Refrigerators were rare in British households before the war. They could be bought on hire purchase, although most people disapproved of paying in this way.

► Middle-class parents were beginning to have smaller families. This meant they could spend more on toys, books and amusements.

▼ Children continued to improvise their own fun. Working-class parents still tended to have large families, so that there was little money for toys.

Leisure

▲Railway companies took advantage of the growing demand for cheap family holidays. Here a station-master on the Southern Railway serves tea to a party inspecting a carriage which has been kitted out as a camping coach. These coaches were placed at country stations or by the sea. They cost 50/– (£2.50) a week to rent.

During the thirties the virtues of healthy exercise and fresh air were emphasised. Most people were able to make an excursion on their Bank Holidays. Whole factories were closed down for a week each summer, and in the North whole towns closed for Wakes Week. The idea was becoming accepted that all workers should have a week's holiday on full pay. A law passed in 1938 added an extra eight million workers to the three million who were already entitled to paid holiday.

To cater for them, seaside holiday camps were opened in competition with boarding-houses. Centres for country walking were popular. The Youth Hostel movement provided cheap accommodation for hikers and cyclists. Railway companies offered special holiday fares, and displayed posters in their carriages and waiting-rooms to promote the resorts. A few better-off families ventured abroad. An eight-day coach tour of the Bavarian Alps cost only 10 guineas (£10.50), including hotel expenses, in 1937.

Increased leisure time brought big crowds of spectators to watch sport. The National Playing Fields Association was formed to improve facilities for people to take part in sports themselves. Record-breaking achievements were widely discussed: Len Hutton scored 364 runs at The Oval in 1938; Sir Malcolm Campbell challenged the water-speed record in his boat *Bluebird*; Fred Perry was successful in the Wimbledon tennis championships, though he turned professional in 1937 and could no longer compete.

Other popular heroes were the dance-band leaders such as Jack Hylton, Ray Noble and Ambrose. Music could now be enjoyed by anyone with access to a wireless or gramophones. People enjoyed jazz and 'swing' from America as well as home-grown revue numbers. Noël Coward's songs were just as popular as sentimental ballads from musicals such as *Lilac Time* and *The Dancing Years*.

◄Golfers enjoying the fresh air of Hertfordshire at the Ashridge Club in 1938. Henry Cotton was a sporting hero of the time, having won the Open Championship in 1937 against strong American challengers. It was a good selling point for the more expensive suburban houses to be near a golf course.

▲A display of barefoot 'natural movement' from a pageant near London in 1936. With cricket, rugger and soccer being played almost exclusively by men, women had to find their own opportunities to keep fit. The Women's League of Health and Beauty encouraged graceful exercise like this.

◀Holiday camps became popular thanks to their welcoming, informal atmosphere. Special events like this piggy-back race were organised for visitors' enjoyment. They made a change from boarding-houses, where holidays could be spoiled by strict rules and nothing to do in bad weather.

▲In 1935 the first Penguin paperback books were published. They made a vast difference to the way people used their leisure: for the first time it became possible to buy good fiction and non-fiction for only 6d. (2½p). For children, new coloured comics appeared, including *Dandy* in 1937 and *Beano* in 1938.

Medical Services

A man who was in work was entitled to medical treatment and any medicines prescribed by his doctor free of charge. But if his wife or children were taken ill, visits to the doctor cost money. On top of a fee of perhaps 7/6 for a visit (37½p) there might be a charge for drugs, so the doctor had to prescribe only what the patient could afford to buy, not necessarily the best.

Hospitals were run by local authorities or by private charity. Funds to staff and equip the wards were raised at bazaars and by Flag Days. This often meant that nurses were badly paid. A hospital bed, or two weeks in a nursing home to have a baby, cost between £6 and £10. But patients did not have to pay to stay in isolation hospitals, where those with an infectious disease were taken to prevent it being passed on to other people.

Dental treatment was expensive. The electric drill was slow, so that a filling took hours. An extraction was made less painful by an injection of cocaine or a whiff of gas. False teeth were too expensive for many people, so they went without.

It was rare to see a hearing-aid. Woolworths sold cheap but inaccurate spectacles. Opticians' glasses ranged from 6/- (30p) to 19/6 for the new bi-focals.

School medical and dental visits could uncover problems but it was not always possible for them to be treated. Many children's ailments were the result of poor diet or damp conditions in their homes.

" Now don't you dare come in here and tell me you think you've got measles."

▲ Cramped, unhygienic housing conditions and a poor diet contributed to the spread of diseases like measles among children. Infectious ailments which cause little concern today could make an undernourished child very ill. Local authorities maintained isolation hospitals, often out of town, to cope with large-scale outbreaks of whooping-cough and scarlet fever. One danger of having to pay for most medical attention was that a sick person who delayed treatment could infect others.

▶ The out-patients' department at Gravesend Hospital in 1939. In the thirties, just over half the population was entitled to free visits to a doctor. National Health insurance was extended to youths aged 14 to 16 in 1938. The really poor, who were receiving public assistance, paid no medical charges. There were school medical inspections without cost, but no provision for children under five.

▲ The cost of invalid aids was far beyond the reach of families on low incomes, as this advertisement shows. There were no free wheelchairs or furniture to enable sick or disabled people to be nursed comfortably at home. Those who needed help to get about had to pay for the necessary equipment, or rely on charity.

▲ Rather than pay for a doctor's advice or visits, people often drew on their own experience to guess what was wrong. There were numerous patent medicines on the market, and advertisements described symptoms in everyday terms. People prescribed medicines for themselves, such as Fynnon's Salts or Bile Beans. It was cheaper to go to a chemist than to a doctor.

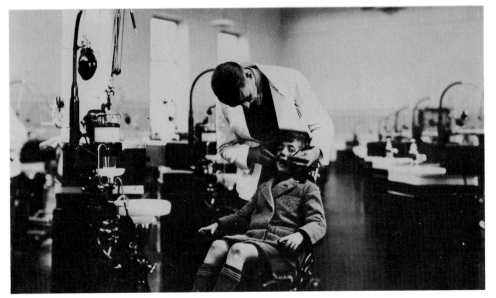

◄ A child patient in the dental clinic at the Royal Free Hospital in London. The treatment given here was much better than that which was generally available. School dental inspections could discover if anything was wrong and advised on what treatment was needed. But the treatment itself could be a painful experience. In many surgeries there were not even facilities for patients to wash out their mouths. The free service was often refused.

11

Evacuation

Britain declared war on Germany on 3 September 1939. It came as no surprise to the British people, for since the Munich crisis of the previous year the country had been preparing for the dreaded aerial attacks by bombs or poison gas. A death toll of 600,000 was forecast for the first three months of war. Nearly two million Anderson-type air-raid shelters were built, and gas masks were issued to 38 million people. Large-scale evacuation of children had been planned since the spring.

It was estimated that about one-third of the country was severely at risk from air raids. Ports, and densely populated manufacturing towns supplying the war effort would be prime targets for the Luftwaffe (the German air force).

Another one-third was a 'neutral' area less likely to be attacked. The remainder of the country, consisting mainly of rural areas, was classed as safe. Evacuees were moved to these reception areas from the towns so as to have the best chance of surviving the bombing.

The official evacuation concentrated on moving school parties. This huge task was begun on Friday, 1 February, the day German troops invaded Poland. Children and their teachers assembled in school playgrounds. The parents who were there to say goodbye had little idea where their children would be sleeping that night. Transport companies worked round the clock for the next few days. moving nearly 1½

▼ London schoolchildren, each wearing an identity label (shown on the inset) and carrying a gas mask, wave to families seeing them off. Many were in holiday mood, ready to make the best of country life.

LONDON COUNTY COUNCIL
JOYCE ARRAM.
'99ᵃ Kentish Town Rd.
ST. PANCRAS, N:
GREAT COLLEGE STREET L.C.C. (I.) SCHOOL,
KENTISH TOWN ROAD, N.W.I.

P.T.O.

million people. At the same time the regular services were crowded with travellers who had made their own arrangements to escape the bombs by leaving cities for the country.

Parents had been urged to register their children for evacuation, though this was not compulsory. But billeting officers in reception areas could require householders to provide foster-homes if they had room. Most children found a warm welcome.

By nightfall, with the new blackout regulations in force, the evacuees were asleep in strange beds after their weary journeys. Many host families were shocked by the obvious poverty of their new guests, which was something they had never seen before.

▲Princess Elizabeth and Princess Margaret Rose broadcasting to the nation's children in October 1940. The King refused to send them away, even after the Palace was bombed.

◀A cartoon by Giles from July 1944. A new wave of evacuation followed the 'doodlebug' attacks of that year (see page 22). Hospitality was now wearing thin.

"Now I want you to promise me you're all going to be really *good* little evacuees and not worry his Lordship."

DON'T do it, mother—

LEAVE THE CHILDREN WHERE THEY ARE

ISSUED BY THE MINISTRY OF HEALTH

▲ This poster urges mothers to keep their children in the country. By the end of October 1939 many were tempted to bring their children home.

◀Evacuees at Fairlawns, Kent in May 1940. During the summer this peaceful county became known as part of 'bomb alley'. Some schools were evacuated again to safer areas.

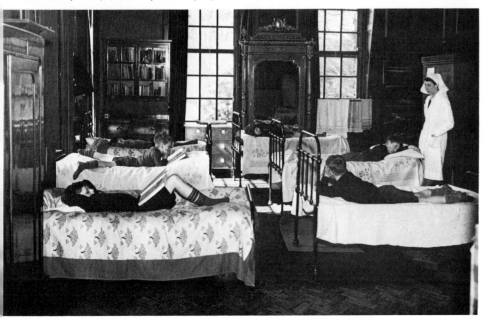

Air Raids

During 1939 and the early months of 1940 hardly any bombs fell. This period came to be called the 'phoney war' or 'bore war'. However, Hitler was planning to invade Britain. Winston Churchill became Prime Minister at this critical time.

The Dunkirk evacuation of the British Expeditionary Force from France, and the fall of France itself, left Britain alone to face invasion. The forerunner of the Home Guard, named the L.D.V., was established but there were few weapons.

Then the bombs began to fall on Britain's airfields. Hitler was determined to destroy the R.A.F. before sending an invasion force across the Channel. The Battle of Britain was fought in the air during the summer of 1940. German bombers then began to bomb London. This was the beginning of the Blitz on civilians, which continued until the following spring.

The first raids on London's East End gave a taste of things to come. All windows were blacked-out, and streets were unlit, so that it was hard for bomber pilots to find their targets. When the first siren sounded, people went down to Underground stations to shelter. After the siren sounded the All-Clear they came up to find familiar streets a mass of rubble.

Each street had an Air Raid Warden, often a man whose ill-health made him unfit for active service. At first Air Raid Wardens were thought to be rather a joke, but when the bombing started people realised how important they were, and the numbers of volunteers increased dramatically. The job of the Air Raid Wardens was to summon fire engines and ambulances, and to check for casualties or unexploded bombs. People whose homes had been bombed or who were in danger from unexploded bombs were moved to rest centres.

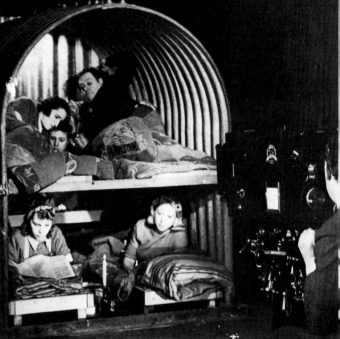

▲ The Ministry of Information was responsible for warning and encouraging people in dangerous war conditions. Here a film is being made of how an Anderson shelter can be fitted with bunk beds to provide as much comfort as possible during air raids.

◄ One of the worst areas of devastation was around St Paul's Cathedral. The building itself survived, although on 12 September 1940 a bomb landed near the foundations. But it failed to explode and was dealt with on Hackney Marshes by a bomb disposal squad.

► Flights of barrage balloons, intended to discourage dive-bombing and low-level attacks, were moored by cables over cities and ports. Crews from R.A.F. Balloon Command fixed them in place. This one is at Coventry, a prime Luftwaffe target.

▲This poster aimed to boost morale, as blackout regulations made the operation of normal services very difficult. The transport system was a prime target for bombers and suffered great damage.

▲From 1940 onwards, Churchill fostered the spirit of national resistance to the aggressor. His speeches calling for unity of purpose were widely broadcast, and posters carried the same message.

▲Buckingham Palace was hit three times between September 1940 and March 1941. The Queen said she could 'now look the East End in the face.'

The G.I.s

▼U.S. aircrew aboard a B-24 Liberator, nicknamed 'Flying Joker'. The British reaction to slogans and nicknames varied; some thought the Americans weren't serious enough, others admired their informal manners and disregard for rank or class.

'Give us the tools and we will finish the job,' Churchill promised early in 1941. The United States was not yet involved in the fighting, but President Roosevelt responded with the Lend-Lease Bill to provide food and arms for Britain whether or not they could be paid for in dollars. Then two acts of aggression that year caused a shift of strength to Britain's advantage. In June, Hitler invaded the Soviet Union, breaking a pact of 1939. In December, Japanese aircraft bombed the American naval base at Pearl Harbor. This brought the Soviet Union and United States into the war on Britain's side against Germany and Italy, who were allied with Japan.

From early 1942, American troops arrived to establish military bases in the British Isles. The presence of 'Yanks' in Britain was generally welcomed. Knowledge of American life had been limited to the cinema versions from Hollywood. The friendliness and efficiency of the G.I.s (so called because all their equipment was labelled 'Government Issue') won them a lot of goodwill. The Americans were sometimes resented for taking over the girls left behind by British servicemen abroad. They were better paid than their British counterparts, and could take for granted luxuries such as chocolate, fruit and ice-cream. The British were unsympathetic to the American colour bar which segregated black soldiers from whites. They often refused to make racial distinctions between the G.I.s off-duty.

In the two years of preparation for the D-Day landings, Anglo-American friendships were made which remained after the end of the war. Many girls left Britain with their G.I. husbands. The Yanks brought to a weary nation a fresh supply of energy and optimism, new slang expressions, a taste for jive, and lots of Coca-Cola.

▲Many British people found the G.I.s amusing, with their strange habit of chewing gum and their incomprehensible slang. However, they were a source of rationed goods, such as chocolate and nylon stockings.

"Dear Momma, in England they drive on the left side of the road . . ."

▲ Processions of Jeeps with apparently endless supplies of petrol roared along British roads at high speeds. Newly-arrived G.I. drivers sometimes forgot that they had to drive on the left, and got lost because road-signs had been taken down to confuse an invading enemy!

► Between January 1944 and D-Day, another three-quarters of a million G.I.s arrived. Off-duty, they were eager to see London's West End, and almost took it over. This is the largest club, Rainbow Corner, which was always crowded.

▼ An American air force sergeant says goodbye to the British aircraftwoman who was his girlfriend. Sad farewells like this were only temporary for many women. About 80,000 'G.I. Brides' later emigrated to America.

▲ Relaxation from the strains of wartime could be found in the dance halls. G.I. escorts solved a problem for young women whose boyfriends were overseas. They could dance with Yanks, rather than with each other or with boys too young for the forces. Few were prejudiced against a partner's race or colour. Violence sometimes erupted between white and black G.I.s, a sad irony in a time when they were fighting on the same side.

17

Wartime Shortages

▼In January 1941 the meat ration was fixed at 1/2 (6p) worth per head per week. Sugar, bacon, tea and fats were early items to be limited. When planning meals, a woman with a large family had to calculate whether she had enough ration coupons as well as counting the cost. She was helped by Lend-Lease shipments of dried egg, evaporated milk and tinned meat from America.

As more and more merchant ships were sunk by the enemy, imports were restricted to essentials. Within Britain too, most factory production was directed towards the war effort. Many items which had been familiar in peacetime were in short supply.

Really vital goods were shared out by rationing. Most people thought the system was fair, although they grumbled about how little food was available. It was shared by weight or by price. The 'points' system gave shoppers a choice of goods. Each item was worth a certain number of points, depending on its availability.

Pig clubs, rabbit-keeping and chicken runs in the garden could provide a tasty supplement to the standard diet. Home-grown vegetables and imported dried milk and eggs helped too. The government kept up a continual flow of 'Food Facts' designed to keep the nation healthy. Babies did especially well on cod liver oil, orange juice and rose-hip syrup. Works canteens, a school meals service and cheap British Restaurants were established.

Utility clothing and furniture was introduced to make the most of limited raw materials. Second-hand shops did good business.

There were special arrangements for families who lost all their possessions in air raids. When one's best china was smashed in a Blitz it was sad to have to replace it by thick white crockery, but better than nothing. There was a shortage of kitchen utensils after millions of aluminium saucepans had been donated as scrap metal for building aircraft.

Many people found 'making-do' a challenge and were proud of their own inventiveness. The most irritating aspect of shortages was the time it took to find a shop with simple items like razor blades or toothbrushes in stock.

▲ The Ministry of Food published suggestions for making rations go further. For some women it was the first chance to find out about nutritional values and vitamin content which they had missed before.

▲ These children have collected bones from kitchen-waste for the war-effort. The Ministry of Supply had a use for everything, from milk-bottle tops to broken crockery. Posters said that one chop-bone could provide cordite for two gun-cartridges!

▲ The 'Dig for Victory' movement involved everyone with access to a plot of land, even office workers in their lunch breaks. This allotment was cultivated in Kensington Gardens, London, in front of the Albert Memorial.

Women at War

One of the most critical shortages was of labour. For the first time in Britain, from December 1941, single women and childless widows aged between 19 and 30 became liable to call-up. They could choose to go into the armed forces – though not as combatants except in anti-aircraft units – or they could choose factory work.

Classed as 'mobile', these women could be sent to manufacturing areas where the need was greatest. They lived in hostels and worked in conditions of noise, dirt and smells that until then were often thought too rough for most women. A total of 800,000 women were taken on in agriculture, local government service, public utilities, transport, shipping and fishing. Some 600,000 men were released to join the forces. Soon all women were 'gainfully employed', apart from mothers of children under 14.

In July 1943 women aged between 46 and 50 were required to register for war work. Called the 'grannies' call-up', this was one of Ernest Bevin's few unpopular decisions during the war.

The manner in which they tackled their new jobs brought about changes in attitudes to working women. A number kept their husbands' private businesses going, from milk rounds to insurance. For physical strength a farmer reckoned three women were about equal to two men.

Even skilled men who reluctantly took on women as their assistants had to admit they were 'not too bad' and could master technical skills with a bit of training.

Every working woman had to do a rtain number of hours each week. Some made the time up by doing two or three part-time jobs, fitting in housework and queuing for the shops in between.

▲Women's magazines printed in colour gravure were popular. *Woman* first appeared in 1937. This copy (left) from 1940 has a civilian cover-girl. By 1942, women in uniform were being illustrated, indicating the change in emphasis from the home to the war effort. The girl shown here is a member of the A.T.S. (Auxiliary Territorial Service), about which a film was made in 1943 (*The Gentle Sex*).

▼Members of the W.V.S. distribute food during the 1941 Coventry Blitz. The W.V.S. (Women's Voluntary Service for Civil Defence) was founded in 1938, and by 1941 had almost a million members. They ran canteens and rest centres, escorted evacuees and organised emergency transport. After major incidents they set up Enquiry Points as well as doing routine tasks behind the scenes.

▲The Women's Land Army, with 80,000 members, had 6,000 in the Timber Corps, felling trees and working in sawmills. These girls had jobs with the Forestry Commission.

◄A.T.S. girls crew an anti-aircraft gun in Kent in 1942. The conscription of women started in December 1941, offering the choice between jobs in industry or the forces.

▼Women's wartime role provided frivolous material for cartoonists. and press photographers, yet their contribution to the war effort was vital.

A. R. P. DEPT.
"I feel sure we could drive a fire engine."

The Last Months

From early 1944, victory was in sight although a 'Little Blitz' added an extra 1,000 dead to those already killed in air raids. Everyone knew that the army was planning a second front to attack German troops in mainland Europe. To speed the landing of Allied troops on the French coast, floating concrete platforms 60 metres long were built, ready to be towed across the Channel. PLUTO, the pipeline under the ocean, was ready to supply oil for the armies after they had landed. Southampton docks were crammed with vessels, and long lines of tanks rumbled towards the South Coast.

A week after the long-awaited and well-prepared D-Day landings on the Normandy coast in June 1944, revenge was speeding towards London. Pilotless aircraft with fiery tails appeared overhead. At first they were greeted with cheers, thought to be enemy aircraft crashing in flames. But they were designed so that when their fuel supply was cut off they plummeted down and exploded with a force rarely experienced before. Casualties were high until people learned to take cover when the engine-noise stopped.

On 8 September a mysterious explosion was heard all over London. Little information was released though Londoners were led to believe that it was caused by a gas leak. As more explosions occurred in the following

READY—STEADY—····

▲ During the spring of 1944, secret preparations for the invasion of Europe were being made. This cartoon of 2 May shows Churchill putting the Allies under starter's orders. Day trips to the South Coast were banned. Tonnes of military equipment were hidden in the Hampshire countryside ready for D-Day on 6 June. Meanwhile dummy tanks and landing craft were parked on the East Coast, to mislead German reconnaissance planes.

▶ 'British fighters sweep hourly across occupied France, cheered by French peasants.' By the end of June, over 850,000 men and 150,000 Allied vehicles had landed in France. The German commander in Paris surrendered on 25 August. The subsequent Allied advance captured V-1 launching sites, bringing a lull in flying-bomb attacks. Some of Hitler's own Colonels attempted to assassinate him, but the plot failed and battles continued through the autumn and winter without much sign that Germany's resistance was weakening.

British fighters sweep hourly across occupied France, cheered by French peasants

months, people joked about 'flying gas mains'. In fact they were due to the second vengeance weapon, a rocket called the V-2. Each one carried a tonne of explosive in its warhead.

In spite of these terrors, there were hopes for peace. A better society was promised to greet the demobilised forces. The Beveridge Report, of which 635,000 copies had been sold, set out possibilities for a new system of social security. With the end of the Battle of the Bulge in January 1945 German forces were entirely on the defensive. By April, Allied soldiers were uncovering the inhuman horror of Nazi concentration camps, and Britain knew the struggle had been worthwhile.

V-2

Pulse jet
Magnetic compasses
Rudder
Servo controls
Master gyro
Compressed air
Fuel tank
Warhead
Fuses

V-1

Fuses
Warhead
Guidance controls
Alcohol tank
Liquid oxygen tank
Motor
Control surfaces

▲ The mood in 1944 was of prevailing optimism. Nobody could predict when the war would end, but there seemed no possibility of defeat. This A.T.S. dance band reflects the cheerful spirit.

◄ The worst horrors of the final year were the attacks by Hitler's 'vengeance weapons'. The V-1 flying bombs arrived overhead at high speed. Then the sinister engine-note cut, and everyone below waited for the explosion as it hit the ground. The V-2 rocket gave no warning.

▼ A V-1 falls on London near Drury Lane. The blinding flash was followed by a tall plume of smoke. By now this was a common sight.

The Victory Election

National celebrations of victory in Europe in May 1945 were followed by debate on the future of the coalition which had governed during the war. Churchill wanted it to continue until Japan surrendered. Clement Attlee, the Labour leader, demanded an early general election, and one was eventually held on 5 July.

Former Cabinet colleagues went into the fray to campaign vigorously against each other. Tories offered Churchill's continued leadership as their main appeal to the electorate. Labour promised to continue controls, to nationalise essential industries which were unwieldy and wearing out, and to introduce a Welfare State. Churchill made a bad mistake by suggesting that Labour would need a kind of secret police to achieve this.

The election was unusual in that it was the first for ten years, and half a generation had never voted before. Many voters were servicemen stationed abroad. There was a long wait while their postal votes were counted, which meant a delay in knowing the result. Many people had changed their address during the war and were not able to vote. In the circumstances it was surprising that as many as 73% of the electorate voted.

On 17 July, Churchill and Attlee met other Allied leaders at the Potsdam conference, and reviewed a victory parade together in Berlin. It was noticed that the British soldiers cheered Attlee as much if not more than Churchill. At home, the press merely wondered about the size of the Tory majority.

The results which were announced on 26 July revealed an unprecedented Labour landslide and left many people shocked. It seemed a rebuff for the leader who had inspired the nation to its finest hour. But for the next six years, Attlee was to lead Britain in an equally heroic struggle towards economic recovery.

◄ Winston Churchill's electioneering tour of Britain in 1945 was greeted with cheers, but these were mainly for the man himself and not for the Conservative Party. Their slogan 'Send him back to finish the job' referred to Churchill's success as a war leader. But publicity from the Labour Party concentrated on policies as well as personalities.

► A Labour Party poster reminded voters that post-war reforms which had been promised by a coalition Committee of Reconstruction still had to be set in motion. The Labour manifesto gave a committment to providing the social security outlined in the Beveridge Plan, public ownership of major industries, full employment and proper housing.

▼ The announcement of the end of the war came on 7 May, when it was declared that the following two days would be public holidays. Celebrations like this one took place all over the country. The official announcement had been awaited since 1 May, when it was learned that Hitler had killed himself in Berlin.

HELP THEM FINISH **THEIR** JOB!
Give them homes and work!
VOTE LABOUR

▲ Mr Attlee campaigned without ceremony, visiting constituencies in a small Austin driven by his wife. In the same manner he went to Buckingham Palace on 26 July to be invited to form a government. Millions of men and women under thirty had voted for the first time, and their votes probably contributed to the Labour landslide victory.

Cinema and Radio

During the war years, regular weekly cinema audiences grew from 20 million to 32 million. Going to the pictures was the most popular form of entertainment. Many towns had a dozen cinemas or more, and patrons could see a different show every night if they wished.

Most films in the forties, especially the 'B' features, were in black and white, so a main feature in Technicolor was a great draw. These were usually supported by Disney cartoons, 'food flashes', travelogues and newsreels. Recitals on the cinema organ were often given at the intervals during advertisements.

Cinemas built before the war, with names like the Majestic, the Alhambra, and Palace, still held glamour and an illusion of living in luxury. The drab, austere world outside could be forgotten for a shilling or two.

At home, the wireless continued to provide family entertainment, general knowledge, and a taste of culture for many who had little formal education. The B.B.C. had been invaluable during the war years. The nine o'clock news, which followed the sonorous chimes of Big Ben, was regarded as utterly trustworthy. A great following grew for *The Brains Trust* and other programmes which spread information in an easy, friendly manner from the set in the living-room. The B.B.C. Light Programme, the forerunner of today's Radio 2, began in 1945. The Third Programme started in 1946, broadcasting classical music, talks and plays each evening.

During 1940, nine million wireless licences were issued. The B.B.C. did much in the following years to diminish class barriers by broadcasting programmes which were universally acceptable. Broadcasting provided a common culture of popular music, humour, news coverage, drama and specialist knowledge which interested many and patronised nobody.

▼ Children were weekly readers of *Radio Fun*, a comic paper with picture stories featuring people whose voices were familiar on the wireless.

▲ Tommy Handley, star of the weekly radio show *ITMA*, relaxing with other members of the cast during rehearsals. The show started life as *It's That Man Again* and was renamed when every national institution became a set of initials. Several of its catch phrases became popular, including 'Can I do you now, Sir?' and 'T.T.F.N.' (Ta Ta For Now).

◄Celia Johnson and Trevor Howard in *Brief Encounter*, a film directed by David Lean and written by Noel Coward. Lean also directed several other British cinema classics, including adaptations of Charles Dickens's books. The film of *Great Expectations* appeared in 1946. Laurence Olivier's *Henry V* was a classic rich in the patriotism felt by audiences in 1944.

▼A new generation of American stars of the screen was being introduced to British cinemagoers. The cover of *Flix*, an English fan magazine, shows Lucille Ball and Desi Arnaz in *Forever Darling*. Bing Crosby, Bob Hope and Dorothy Lamour starred in light-hearted films, but the box-office draw of all time was the Hollywood epic *Gone with the Wind*.

◄Queuing for William Wyler's *The Best Years of Our Lives* outside London's Leicester Square Cinema in 1946. The film starred Virginia Mayo and Hoagy Carmichael. Notice that West End ticket prices were 7/6 (37½p) or 6/– (30p). Cinema admission in the suburbs and the provinces was much cheaper. The best seats were usually only 2/9 (13½p).

Post-War Austerity

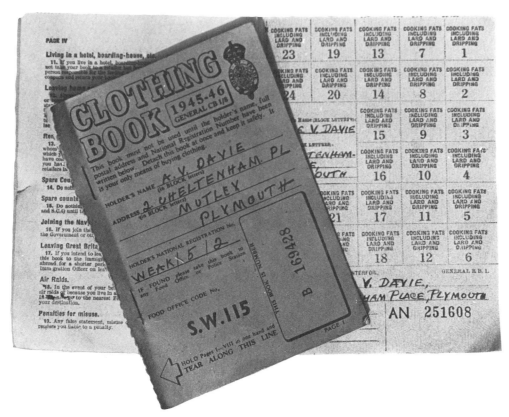

▲Examples of the ration books which continued to clutter pockets and handbags for several years after the war. Even bread and potatoes were rationed for a time. Clothing coupons were sometimes sold on the black market as one coupon was needed even to buy a handkerchief. Clothes came off the ration in 1949 but food rationing did not finally end until 1954.

▼Queuing for new shoes at an annual sale in January 1949. Notice the dilapidated shop front. Quite apart from shortages, prices were rising rapidly. It was accepted that after a two-hour wait in the cold, customers might reach the front of the queue and find an empty shop. Shoe-menders were always short of leather, and they were sure of finding buyers for any uncollected repairs.

The end of the Lend-Lease agreement with America after the war provoked a balance-of-payments crisis in Britain. The United States granted a loan of 3.75 billion dollars, and Britain had to put her energies into producing goods for export. At the same time money had to be found to rebuild the shattered cities and ports, to house many thousands of homeless families, and to invest in run-down major industries.

The tremendous export effort created ironies for working people. Before the war they had not been able to afford luxuries. Now they enjoyed better wage levels, but there were no luxuries on sale in the shops. An exhibition of goods was rousingly named 'Britain Can Make It'. Almost every item bore a label saying 'For Export Only', and visitors added the bitter comment 'But Britain can't have it!'

The coal industry was nationalised on 1 January 1947. Later that same winter a fuel crisis paralysed the country for several weeks. This had nothing to do with nationalisation. It was bitterly cold and Emanuel Shinwell, Minister of Fuel, had not alerted people sufficiently to the dwindling supplies.

From the last week in January until mid-March, heavy snow blocked road and rail communications so that stocks could not be moved. Power cuts affected homes and places of work. Production fell as raw materials could not be delivered, and people were unable to get to work. A thaw in March put an end to the fuel crisis but caused widespread flooding. As well as causing damage to property, this left farmland too waterlogged to plough in time for a good harvest.

Try **BARRACOUTA** for breakfast!

Delicious Fish Cakes

Psst!

▲ The 'spiv' in his zoot suit, mocking austerity, was famous for being able to lay hands on goods in short supply, and would sell them at a price. Consignments of luxuries intended for export were re-routed mysteriously for cash, it was claimed, and the pavement salesman could supply goods, such as nylons, bananas, chocolates and ice-cream.

Fish Cakes

These can be made overnight and re-heated.

Ingredients: 1 can barracouta, 8 oz. mashed potatoes, 2 level tablespoons finely chopped onion, 1 level teaspoon thyme, salt and pepper

BARRACOUTA is helping out with breakfast in many homes to-day. This economical smoked fish, now off points, makes tempting and savoury dishes such as Fish Cakes and Toasts. Barracouta comes in 1½ lb. cans, price 1/-. All recipes are for four people.

Barracouta Fritters

Ingredients: 4 oz. self-raising flour *or* 4 oz.

▲ In a desperate attempt to relieve monotony in family diets, the Government tried to persuade shoppers to try alternatives. Canned barracouta and snoek were imported, but did not catch on. A campaign to popularise whalemeat was not a success, and most people just ate less of what they were used to.

◀ Homeless families were sometimes accommodated in 'pre-fabs' which were delivered in sections and could be erected on site in about four hours. This gave the occupiers a plot of land as well, being used here to grow vegetables and raise chickens.

▼ In the chaos caused by bad weather in March 1947, these Londoners are shovelling snow. The exercise at least kept them warm. Most homes were enduring long power cuts and the coalman had stopped calling months before. At work it was no better: many factories had shut for lack of fuel.

Dawn of Recovery

Two years after Victory, there still seemed no end to drabness in fashion and food. Even bread and potatoes were rationed. Dressmakers could be taken to court for embroidering garments, and tailors were fined for providing more pockets or bigger cuffs than regulations allowed. In the Potteries, china was being decorated illegally in private homes.

People were growing weary of petty restrictions. Even the newspapers reporting these minor breaches of the law were limited in size. Private builders needed licences to build homes for sale and had to tackle a daunting quantity of paperwork to do small repairs. The basic petrol ration was abolished, putting an end to pleasure motoring.

In the spring of 1947 Dior's 'New Look' was launched on the fashion scene, and spread rapidly from Paris to a Britain starved of glamour. Within a year it was seen everywhere, provoking a puritanical outcry about its extra-vagant use of material. Women appeared elegantly clad once more against the grey background of empty shops and lingering bomb damage. Mass production saw to it that voluminous coats, plunging necklines and swirling hems could be made widely available. They provided a taste of luxury in every High Street, and renewed hope for the end of austerity and controls.

On cleared bomb-sites, attempts to cope with the housing shortage resulted in colonies of 'pre-fabs'. Organised groups of squatters took over empty Nissen huts in the vacated Army camps, having nowhere else to live.

Long-term plans to raise standards of housing, and to reduce the numbers of homeless people, had been introduced in the New Towns Bill of April 1946. These plans, when put into practice, would transfer whole communities to spacious new estates, providing new jobs in new factories.

December 29, 1945—ILLUSTRATED

"*Look!*
MY KITCHEN'S ALL SHINY
IN NO TIME AT ALL
*now I've gone modern
with* MIRRO!"

Mirro's special detergent cuts grease and sticky scum in seconds. **Buy an 8d.** giant canister of this "screen-sifted" non-scratch cleanser to-day.

Go Modern
WITH
MIRRO
THE SAFE, SPEEDY CLEANSER

THOMAS HEDLEY AND COMPANY LIMITED. NEWCASTLE-ON-TYNE

▲ Notice the 'no coupons' label on this advertisement. A woman's role was changing and she could combine homemaking with a career. The market in domestic labour-saving products boomed while stainless steel and plastic eased kitchen chores.

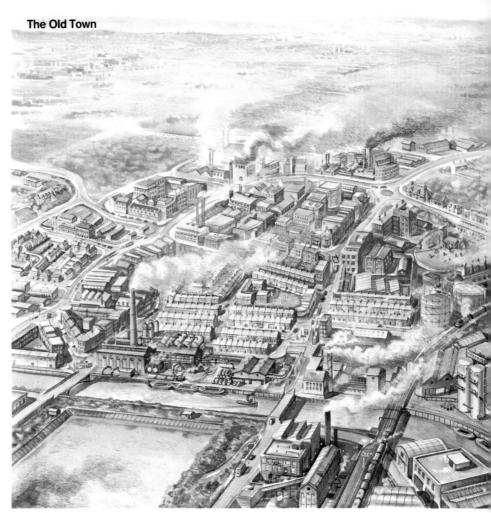

The Old Town

JAEGER

The best in Utility

YOU CAN BUY JAEGER UTILITY EVERYWHERE

Vogue Jan. 1944.

Utility and the New Look

◀ The Board of Trade had introduced the 'Utility' standard in clothing manufacture. This was supposed to ensure that poorer people could afford to buy clothes, and that production concentrated on cheap, practical and hard-wearing materials and designs. Quality was standardised, and the prevailing taste was for square shoulders and straight lines.

▶ The 'New Look' was shapelier, a brave return to graceful shoulders, curves, narrow waists and long swirling skirts. Hips were emphasised by padding or the wearing of stiff petticoats underneath.

Women rejoiced in the luxury of feeling feminine again; girls, for the first time, could dress for fun rather than for efficiency and economy.

MADE IN ENGLAND from TESCAN Fur Skins

The New Town

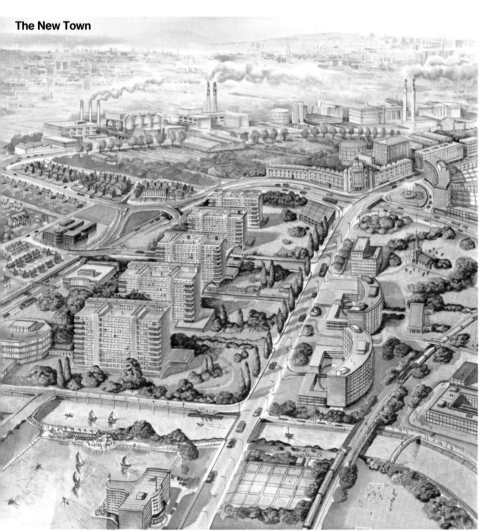

◀ The old, industrial city contrasted with a new, planned townscape which was intended to replace it. Planners of the forties had high hopes for large blocks of flats with pleasant green spaces in between. In practice they were often found to be inhuman in scale. Many people later looked back with affection on the cosy terraces which in the past had seemed only cramped and mean.

The Old Town
1. Pre-war factories had been built without urban planning, wherever land was cheap.
2. Roads were too narrow for modern traffic.
3. Terraced streets were often dark and airless, hastily constructed and without gardens.
4. Churches had been overshadowed by industrial buildings.
5. Schools were cramped and dingy, playgrounds were few and badly laid out.
6. Rivers were polluted. Rarely used now for barge transport, they flowed between neglected wharves.

The New Town
7. New factories were to be sited away from dwellings, both for health and efficiency.
8. Roads were to be widened, and ring roads built to keep traffic out of city centres.
9. Multi-storey flats were to be erected in parkland surroundings of light and space.
10. Small houses with their own gardens were to be laid out according to an overall plan.
11. Churches were to be restored and their garden surroundings recreated.
12. Shopping centres and administrative buildings were to be grouped in a single complex.
13. Schools and health centres were to be spacious and set in the open air.
14. Rivers were to be reclaimed, their banks beautified with trees and promenades.

Nationalisation

Private enterprise had pioneered the major industries of Britain, but World War Two had left them very short of capital investment and with outmoded methods and equipment. The Labour Party won massive support with its plans for public ownership. People felt that coal, gas, electricity, and iron and steel were too important to be left in the hands of private companies.

Transport by road and rail could be organised to advantage on a national scale. The state was prepared to invest in a programme of modernisation, and many grievances felt by workers against bosses might be resolved if industry could belong to the people as a whole. New national boards or corporations were to be set up to take over and administer a wide and complex variety of firms.

There was little opposition to these plans except in the case of iron and steel, which was making a profit for the owners. New Year's Day 1947 saw the coal mines brought into public ownership. A year later British Railways came into being, unifying the four big railway companies, which had existed since the twenties.

The British Electricity Authority took overall control of 550 local undertakings. The Road Haulage Executive of the Transport Commission had the task of harmonising the activities of 3,000 firms. Although there were strong political motives for state control, the chief need was to launch a rescue operation in the nation's economic distress.

Britain in debt could not afford anything other than the most efficient economy possible, and all workers in the public and the private sector were given production targets. 'Output Per Man-Hour' challenges were issued. Trade union members were to be consulted at all levels in the newly-nationalised industries, which employed nearly a quarter of the workforce, improving the status of trade unions.

▼ Austin cars for export being loaded at London Docks. Over 70% of the output of private cars in the late forties was exported. New markets were being established overseas while the home market was deliberately kept short. The industrial wage-earner was in full employment, often with high rates of overtime pay. But since so many goods were being shipped abroad there was little to buy. The export drive resulted in 'too much money chasing too few goods'.

HE STOOPS TO CONQUER

▲ This cartoon shows a miner supporting British industry. Miners' wages doubled between 1939 and 1945, but despite increased mechanisation productivity had declined. The task facing the National Coal Board was huge.

► The struggle for union recognition had been bitterly fought in the pits, and local ceremonies greeted nationalisation. However, the fuel crisis still meant that thousands of workers were laid off.

▼ A cartoon pokes fun at the idea that nationalisation meant true ownership by everyone. Station waiting-rooms were as cold as ever!

▲ 'Mr. Cube' in fighting mood! By 1950 labour leaders were advocating a less drastic approach to nationalisation. Tate and Lyle's 'Mr Cube' fought off state intervention in sugar refining. In the years which followed, the tide of opinion turned against public ownership and some industries returned to private control.

The Welfare State

During the war years, posters and publicity continued to raise the level of public health. There was increased awareness of nutritional needs and of the value of vitamins in a balanced diet. Campaigns to encourage vaccination and immunisation helped to stamp out pre-war diseases such as diphtheria. In 1956 there were only 53 cases compared to 65,000 in 1938.

On 5 July 1948 the National Health Service came into being. One of its chief pioneers, Aneurin Bevan, called it 'an act of collective goodwill and public enterprise'. It made medical care a social right, not a private commodity to be bought and sold. At the same time a new National Assistance Act came into effect to combine a range of benefits and entitlements in one full, comprehensive insurance scheme.

If cost had previously been a deterrent to patients needing a doctor or dentist there was now no bar to their asking for treatment. The same applied to those needing hearing-aids, glasses or false teeth, which would be given free.

The rush on these items in the first months was not a signal that the system would be expensively abused, but evidence of past neglect. For example, the problem of deafness had never been

tackled thoroughly. The N.H.S. had a hearing aid designed and mass-produced, and by 1951 it had been distributed to 150,000 grateful users.

There was some opposition to the scheme from the doctors' association, the British Medical Association. This was eventually overcome and many doctors, especially in the provinces, welcomed the wider availability of specialists and consultants who had previously been in private practice in London. The N.H.S. was to be paid for mainly out of taxation, with a small National Insurance contribution. The new service cost a great deal. Doctors wrote 187 million prescriptions for medicines, and the annual N.H.S. bill was over £50 million.

Other benefits were covered by the individual National Insurance contributions paid by everyone of working

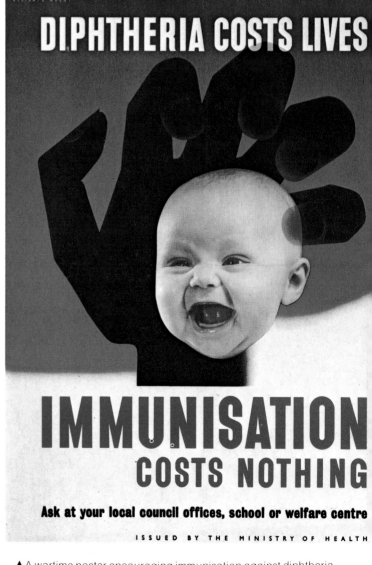

▲A wartime poster encouraging immunisation against diphtheria.

age. Benefits varied in accordance with the class of the contributor. A self-employed person, for example, was not entitled to unemployment benefit but could claim National Assistance. Everyone had to join, including the 'bosses' and the non-employed. This fairness, and the idea that individuals could now expect to be cared for 'from the cradle to the grave' made the new provisions popular and they were the admiration of the rest of the world.

▶ Continuing emphasis on stepping-up production and the greater employment of women led to more welfare services and better conditions at work. Staff canteens, such as this one, were offering cut-price or free refreshments and there were improved washing facilities. Larger factories sometimes acquired sports grounds.

"Dentist says if there are any more of you thinking of fitting one another up with National Health teeth for Christmas presents you've had it."

◀ A Giles cartoon of 1949. The National Health Service provided free false teeth, spectacles, wigs, artificial limbs and hearing aids. Although this caught the imagination of cartoonists it was of enormous practical benefit to those who could not otherwise have afforded them. 5,250,000 pairs of spectacles were issued in the first year. The cost of the scheme meant some charges were later re-introduced. It became almost as difficult to make a dental appointment as to buy a motor car.

▶ New school building featured large in public expenditure to cope with the new Tripartite system for secondary education which included Grammar, Technical and Modern schools. The school-leaving age was raised to 15, and the bulge in the birth-rate meant that more children had to be accommodated. This is a new junior school of 1950. Schools were being designed to be spacious and airy, with more light and colour than before. Five thousand schools had been damaged in air raids but by the summer of 1949 new school places were being provided at the rate of 300 per week.

The Family Car

Petrol was rationed during and after the war, and there was strict control on the number of cars manufactured for the home market. Nevertheless motor car ownership in Britain grew from 1.7 million in 1938 to 4.4 million in 1950. The vehicle industry began to expand along with others after factory space and machinery were converted from war work to peacetime production.

Harlow New Town was being planned in 1947, to increase Harlow's population from 4,500 to 90,000. At that time one garage was allowed for every ten dwellings, but by the time it was half-built estimates were revised to provide one garage for every two households. During the fifties, car ownership was to double. Such a large change threatened the economy of public transport services and had permanent effects on the environment.

Cars produced in the immediate post-war years looked very much like those of 1939 and before. But soon there were new and better designs which took advantage of mass-production methods to supply efficient family cars at reasonable prices. The motoring boom continued as petrol rationing ended. Credit became more easily available for hire purchase and, with nearly full employment, manual workers managed to increase their wages through trade union negotiations to compare favourably with 'white collar' pay.

A small saloon contained thousands of component parts, and the car industry's success generated employment. Gradually the many small manufacturers were reduced to a few main producers. Austin and Morris were merged in 1952.

Most families looked forward to buying their own car. The freedom to drive in any direction you chose, whenever you wanted to, was something that the older generation had hardly imagined.

▲Children practising for a Road Safety demonstration at a National Safety First Congress to be held at Westminster. The Road Traffic Act of 1934 had introduced driving tests for motorists, and a year later a 30 m.p.h. speed limit was imposed in built-up areas. With the amount of traffic growing fast there were still too many road accidents. There was an increasing need for children to know and follow the Highway Code.

▼A picnic at Leith Hill in 1946. Leisure motoring was restricted during the war and by post-war austerity, but a family car gave people who could save their basic petrol ration a chance to explore the countryside. It was a time when 'Holidays At Home' were encouraged. Restrictions on foreign currency allowances meant that even better-off people had few opportunities to travel abroad. Instead, they drove to quiet parts of Britain.

◄ Cleaning the family car outside the suburban home became a regular ritual. Before private transport came to be taken for granted, a few cynical commentators concluded that working people thought of cars as 'status symbols'. But they were more likely to have been bought for practical reasons, such as carrying shopping or holiday luggage, visiting relatives, or going to work, school, clubs and meetings.

SEE THE SENSATIONAL NEW
AUSTIN '10'

Generous power and modern construction give exceptional performance under
FULL FAMILY LOAD

Every expert who has driven the new Austin '10' has been enthusiastic about its appearance and performance. High power to-weight ratio, and unified body-and-chassis construction give smoother, safer riding with livelier acceleration and greater power.

See these models at your Agents or at Austin's London Showrooms, 479 Oxford St., W.1

Spacious Interior. Look at the wide doorways which make for easy entrance, and the big air back-and-enter-yourself seats. The screen, side and rear windows are all of toughened safety glass.

FIXED-HEAD SALOON	£175
SLIDING-HEAD SALOON	£185
OPEN FOUR-SEATER	£175

INVEST IN AN AUSTIN—THE CAREFREE CAR

▲ The Austin 10 of 1939 cost £175 and was a general favourite. It was built to last, and production re-started after the war, so thousands were still on the road in the late forties.

◄ The revolutionary Morris Oxford appeared in 1948, challenging upright designs with its more rounded appearance. Notice the wide radiator and recessed headlamps.

327 FC

Festival of Britain

Among the uncleared ruins of war, the idea was born that Britain needed a morale-boost. The idea of a Festival took shape in the harsh post-war years of economy. A hundred years earlier, Victorians had marvelled at the Great Exhibition. From May to September 1951 another display of national prowess drew millions of sightseers.

Londoners had a year in which to watch curious shapes rising on the South Bank of the Thames, and to wonder what the end result would be. The Dome of Discovery and the Skylon were dismantled at the end of the exhibition; the only permanent structure was the Royal Festival Hall. There were cries of outrage about the waste of scarce raw materials. Some journalists said it was a political stunt by Herbert Morrison, who was nicknamed 'Lord Festival'.

The organisers worked for 'a year of fun, fantasy and colour, a year in which we can, while soberly surveying our great past and our promising future, for once let ourselves go.' Designers did indeed let themselves go. Glass, concrete, plastics, wood showing its natural grain, bright colours and sparkling aluminium were combined to give cheerful illusions of light and space. Included in the exhibition were yet more inspired designs in a style which became known as 'contemporary'.

The Exhibition portrayed the autobiography of a nation, the land and the people. Upstream was the theme of the land, its minerals and agriculture; downstream the people whose character developed its rich diversity. Visitors could begin with the Country pavilion or the Natural Scene and move through to Power and Production, Transport and Britain's Ancestry. In the Lion and Unicorn pavilion the traditions which had shaped social history were featured, including British eccentricities. One of these, Roland Emett's railway, was built in the Pleasure Gardens.

◄ Most magazines commemorated the Festival of Britain with a souvenir issue. Some took a serious approach, concentrating on Britain's economic achievements. Others, like this issue of *Blighty*, emphasised the gaiety and fun to be experienced in the fairground built for the Festival in Battersea Park.

▼ The site chosen for the South Bank exhibition took full advantage of the effect created by night-time illuminations reflected in the river. Lighting increased the futuristic impact of the Skylon and the Dome of Discovery for visitors taking a trip by boat along the river.

▲ The Conveyancer D6-20 fork-lift truck could carry loads of 6,000 lbs (2,722 kg) at speeds between 0 and 9 m.p.h. Such exhibits were reminders that Britain was still an inventive pioneer in industrial technology.

▲ The Festival provided a showcase for the new wave of industrial designers who came to influence taste when austerity was on the wane. This is a design for Shelley Potteries 'Symphony' crockery.

▼ Not all new design was greeted with reverence. This Murphy wooden radio cabinet of 1949 was nicknamed 'The Commode'. One visitor found the whole Festival too much: 'The mind boggled and the feet gave out.'

▲ Souvenir manufacture flourished, offering Festival ties, ashtrays, novelty 'slipper-sox', commemorative soap, and sticks of rock (in exchange for sweet coupons, of course). This plastic paperweight shows the jaunty official symbol, Britannia in profile, poised for a new age, a rising star with a hint of patriotic bunting. Plastic seemed to be the material of the future, with endless possibilities.

Looking Back

At 11.15 a.m. on 6 February 1952 a black-bordered newspaper came on sale in London's streets. With powerful simplicity it announced that the King had died in his sleep.

People at home and abroad were deeply shocked. From all over Britain, those who had endured the national hardships characterising the reign of George VI came to pay tribute to a dedicated family man who had been trained for service, but not for monarchy. As Duke of York, he had established camps where boys from public schools could meet and mix with working-class boys.

The events of his reign toppled social barriers by bringing people together in air raid shelters, army camps and queues for shops. Now they queued for hours in the rain to pay respect at his lying-in-state.

▲ A Coronation tea-party in Nottingham, 1937.

1936
German troops entered the Rhineland.
The Spanish army mounted a right-wing revolt against the Popular Front government, beginning the Civil War.
Oswald Moseley led an anti-Jewish march through London's East End, where it met with opposition.
Workers from Jarrow staged their Hunger March.
King Edward VIII abdicated in order to marry Mrs. Simpson.
Billy Butlin opened his holiday camp at Skegness.

1937
Spanish rebels, helped by Italian troops, took the city of Malaga in southern Spain; the Basque town of Guernica was bombed by the rebels.
Neville Chamberlain succeeded Baldwin as Prime Minister of Britain.
King George VI was crowned; the event was commemorated by the L.M.S. Railway's new express 'The Coronation Scot'.
The Air Raid Precautions Act became law in Britain.
Britain's Foreign Secretary, Lord Halifax, visited Hitler in Germany to make peace overtures.

1938
A week's holiday with pay was proposed in Britain as a national standard.
The Women's Voluntary Service was founded.
The S.S. *Queen Elizabeth* was launched.
The magazine *Picture Post* started publication.
Walter Runciman, a British official, visited Czechoslovakia and reported in favour of Nazi demands.
Chamberlain visited Hitler on 15 September hoping to prevent war, and again two weeks later at Munich where he agreed to Hitler's demands.

1939
Britain recognised Franco's government in Spain.
The Spanish Civil War ended.
Britain and France pledged support to Poland and guaranteed independence to Roumania and Greece.
Churchill urged a British alliance with the Soviet Union; a German-Soviet pact was signed.
Parliament approved an Emergency Powers Bill.
Hitler's troops invaded Poland on 1 September; France and Britain declared war on Germany on 3 September; 158,000 British troops were sent to fight in France.

1940
British merchant ships totalling 2,725,000 tonnes were sunk.
Food rationing began in Britain; Lord Woolton was made Minister of Food.
Germany invaded Norway and Denmark; then Holland, Luxembourg and Belgium.
Chamberlain resigned as Prime Minister, and Churchill formed a National Government.
British troops were evacuated from Dunkirk.
The German air force failed to defeat the R.A.F. in the Battle of Britain.
Large-scale bombing of Britain began.

▲ V-1 damage in South-East England, 1944.

1941
The U.S. Congress approved the Lend-Lease Bill which gave dollar support to Britain's war effort.
Air-raids and U-boat attacks continued.
Fighting continued in North Africa; German troops attacked Tobruk.
Germany invaded the Soviet Union; Britain and the Soviet Union agreed a mutual assistance pact.
Clothes rationing began in Britain.
Conscription started for single women under 30.
Japanese aircraft bombed the U.S. naval base at Pearl Harbor; America declared war.

1942
Clement Attlee became Deputy Prime Minister.
American forces arrived in Britain to establish military bases.
The German air force began its 'Baedeker' raids, directed against Britain's architectural heritage.
The British Army halted Germany's advance across North Africa at the Battle of el Alamein.
The Beveridge report on Social Security in Britain was published.
Britain began to suffer acute shortages of goods and food; white bread was banned and there was only a limited supply of Utility goods.

1943
Russian troops defeated the German attack at Stalingrad.
The R.A.F. raided Berlin.
Churchill broadcast on post-war reconstruction.
Mussolini fell from power in Italy, which was invaded by the Allies.
Soviet troops took back territory captured by the Germans.
Churchill, Roosevelt and Stalin met to plan the final overthrow of Germany.
Italy surrendered unconditionally to the Allies and declared war on Germany.

▲ Buying nylon stockings, a rare delight in 1946.

1944
The Education Act became law.
Pay-as-you-earn income tax was introduced.
Penicillin was widely used for the first time.
Allied troops were massed on the South Coast in preparation for the D-Day landings.
The first V-1 flying bomb landed on London.
German army officers attempted to assassinate Hitler.
The first V-2 rocket landed in Britain.
German forces managed to halt the Allies' advance at Arnhem in Holland and in the Ardennes in Belgium.

1945
Churchill, Roosevelt and Stalin met at Yalta to decide on future areas of influence in Europe.
Hitler died in Berlin.
Germany surrendered: V.E. Day celebrated on 8 May.
The British general election resulted in a landslide victory: Labour 393 seats, Conservatives 213, Liberals 12; Others 22; Attlee became Prime Minister.
The United States dropped atomic bombs on the Japanese cities of Hiroshima and Nagasaki.
Japan surrendered on 14 August; the war ended.

1946
The British government took emergency powers to deal with the balance-of-payments crisis.
The United Nations General Assembly met.
Leading Nazis were sentenced to death at the War Crimes trials at Nuremberg.
The Bank of England was nationalised.
Bread rationing began in Britain.
The Reith Committee reported, recommending that new towns should be built.
A Royal Commission reported in favour of equal pay for women.

1947
The coal industry was nationalised in Britain.
Britain suffered a severe fuel crisis; newspapers were reduced in size to conserve supplies.
The 'New Look' Dior fashion collection was shown in Paris.
U.S. Secretary of State George Marshall proposed a plan for European recovery (Marshall Aid).
British rule ended in India; the independent states of India and Pakistan were formed.
Princess Elizabeth married Lieutenant Philip Mountbatten.

1948
British railways were nationalised.
The Soviet Union blockaded West Berlin; supplies to the city were airlifted in.
The free National Health Service began operating in Britain.
The British Citizenship Act became law, making Commonwealth citizens British subjects.
Chinese Communists announced that a North China People's Republic had been established.
The Korean People's Democratic Republic was established in North Korea, claiming the whole of Korea for Communism.

1949
The North Atlantic Treaty Organisation (NATO) was founded for mutual assistance against aggression.
Britain recognised the Irish Republic.
Apartheid was introduced in South Africa.
British dockers went on strike and railway workers mounted a 'go slow'.
The pound was devalued from $4.03 to $2.80 causing devaluation of other European currencies.
Nationalisation of the iron and steel industry came into force.

1950
Britain recognised the Communist government in China.
Riots against apartheid occurred in South Africa.
A general election in Britain severely reduced the Labour majority.
The Soviet Union announced that it had atomic bombs; the spy Klaus Fuchs was found guilty of betraying atomic secrets to the Soviet Union.
North Korean forces invaded South Korea.
National Service in Britain was extended to two years.
Marshall Aid to Britain came to an end.

1951
Charges were imposed for services under the National Health Service in order to pay for increased defence spending; Aneurin Bevan resigned from the Cabinet in protest.
The Festival of Britain ran throughout the summer.
Foreign Office officials Burgess and Maclean fled to Russia just before it was discovered that they had been acting as Soviet spies.
The Conservatives won the British general election; Churchill became Prime Minister.
The X-certificate for films was introduced.

1952
King George VI died; Queen Elizabeth II acceded to the throne.
Churchill announced that Britain had produced an atomic bomb.
Cold War over Germany's frontiers intensified.
Trams were withdrawn from service in London.
The British iron and steel industry was de-nationalised.
General Eisenhower won the election for President of the United States.
The world's first hydrogen bomb was exploded by the United States.

1953
Josef Stalin died.
The British road transport industry was de-nationalised.
The summit of Mount Everest was reached for the first time.
Queen Elizabeth II was crowned at a ceremony in Westminster Abbey.
The Soviet Union exploded a hydrogen bomb.
The Korean war ended.
Britain entertained the Commonwealth prime ministers in London.
Britain won the Ashes from Australia.

▲ The end of an era, 1952.

A New Age

▲ The Coronation was a memorable spectacle. The press had a field day, reporting colourful arrivals of heads of state from the Commonwealth, and publishing maps of the processional route and pictures of the regalia. Again, the souvenir industry did well with products ranging from model Coronation coaches to traditional mugs, and new-age plastic ball-point pens. A crowd of 50,000 tried to find places to sleep in the Mall the night before, and even more stood to cheer the newly crowned young Queen when she appeared on the balcony of Buckingham Palace. In millions of homes, the intimate close-up coverage of an awe-inspiring coronation service in Westminster Abbey brought modest suburbia in touch with historic ceremony, and proved the value of television.

Queen Elizabeth II was crowned amid unprecedented pageantry on 2 June 1953. The ancient ceremony demanded that it should be performed 'in the sight of all the people'. On this occasion the feat was more or less achieved, as over 20 million viewers were able to witness the solemn moment on nearly $2\frac{3}{4}$ million television sets. Demand had been increasing rapidly during months of preparation, and people were able to share the excitement through the startlingly clear images on the small screens in their own homes.

The B.B.C. had opened a regular television service in 1936, just before the accession of the Queen's father. It was suspended during the war, but resumed in 1946 with fewer than 12,000 viewers. By 1950 the first regional transmitter was operating from Sutton Coldfield in the Midlands. In this area, made prosperous by motor manufacture, television now became a dominant factor in daily life.

Television was perhaps to be the most far-reaching and important influence on the New Elizabethan age. It brought pictorial immediacy to world news, political, industrial, environmental and social problems, and a wider range of culture, entertainment and sports than was ever accessible before.

New Elizabethans had much to cheer on Coronation Day. Most rationing controls had ended. The Korean War had involved heavy defence spending and interrupted the careers of young men with continuance of National Service, but now it was over. Inflation was almost at a standstill, with a fall in the cost of imported raw materials. Standards of living were rising and the Welfare State was pledged to meet the cost of personal misfortune. Churchill, nostalgically, was back in office. And, as a symbol of the long struggle, Everest was conquered.

▲ The fireside began to share its place at the centre of family life with the new television set. It was a welcome novelty, though at first there was only one channel and programmes were in black and white.

► Larry the Lamb and Muffin the Mule were just two of the characters brought to life by television. Comics like these were quick to cash in on the popularity of particular shows and personalities.

▲ Two BBC announcers in front of the camera, 1950. Critics claimed that television would 'ruin eyesight', 'interfere with homework' and 'ruin the art of conversation'.

► Firms manufacturing receivers vied for custom as regional transmitters extended the range of potential sales. Sets could be rented, or bought on hire purchase as credit eased.

Who was Who

▲ Ernest Bevin: 'Our Ernie' in the factories.

Attlee, Clement R. (1883–1967)
Prime Minister in the post-war Labour government from 1945 to 1951. He was called to the Bar in 1906, and lived for 14 years in London's East End where he became manager of a boys' club and eventually a lecturer at the London School of Economics. From 1922 he was M.P. for Limehouse. He became leader of the Labour Party in 1935 and served as Deputy Prime Minister in the wartime coalition.

Beaverbrook (Lord) (1879–1964)
A millionaire newspaper owner and government minister. Born in Canada as Maxwell Aitken, he made his fortune there before settling in England in 1910. He became a Conservative M.P. and in 1917 received a peerage. Between the wars he gained control of the *Daily Express* and founded the *Sunday Express*, through which he influenced British politics. He was appointed Minister of Aircraft Production in the wartime cabinet.

Bevan, Aneurin (1897–1960)
A miner's son, born in Tredegar in South Wales, he left school at 13 and was largely self-taught. He opposed World War One, denouncing it as a 'capitalist' war. In 1921 he completed two years at the Central Labour College, London, and afterwards was active on behalf of the miners. From 1929 he was M.P. for Ebbw Vale, which he represented until he died. As Minister of Health he inaugurated the N.H.S.

Beveridge (Lord) (1869–1940)
A civil servant and academic, William Beveridge became well known for the report of the Committee on Social Insurance and Allied Services (the Beveridge Report) published in 1941. He left the civil service in 1919 to become director of the London School of Economics. From 1938 he served as warden of University College, Oxford until elected as a Liberal M.P. in 1944. He was knighted in 1919 and received a peerage in 1946.

Bevin, Ernest (1881–1951)
Trade unionist and Labour politician. Born in Somerset, he started his working life as a farm labourer and van driver. By 1911 he was an official of the Dockers' Union. He played a large part in setting up the Transport and General Workers' Union, and was its General Secretary from 1921 to 1940. He became Minister of Labour in the wartime government and was Foreign Secretary in the post-war government.

Chamberlain, Arthur Neville (1869–1940)
Prime Minister from 1937 to 1940. Born in Birmingham and educated at Rugby School, he became Lord Mayor of Birmingham in 1915. In 1918 he entered Parliament as a Conservative, and served as Postmaster-General, Minister of Health and Chancellor of the Exchequer. As Prime Minister, his controversial appeasement policy towards Nazi Germany led to the Munich agreement, but he did not resign until May 1940.

Churchill, Winston (1874–1965)
Prime Minister from 1941 to 1945, and again from 1951 to 1955. Entering Parliament in 1900 as a Conservative, he joined the Liberals in 1908 and served in the Liberal government. After leaving the Liberal Party again he returned to Parliament in 1924, remaining an M.P. until he died. He was a prolific writer, and won the Nobel Prize for literature in 1953. He was knighted in the same year.

Coward, Noël (1899–1973)
Actor, dramatist and composer. He first appeared on stage at the age of 11, and his first play *The Young Idea* appeared in 1921. One of his most popular works *Cavalcade* opened in 1931 and told the story of a middle-class family from the turn of the century, and his film *This Happy Breed* traced social changes between the wars. His mocking song *Don't Let's be Beastly to the Germans* was banned during the war.

Cripps, Stafford (1889–1952)
Labour Chancellor of the Exchequer from 1947. He studied law at London University and was called to the Bar in 1913. During World War One he ran Britain's largest explosives factory. He was knighted in 1930 and elected as a Labour M.P. the following year. He became ambassador to Moscow in 1940. He was a teetotaller and vegetarian, and as Minister of Aircraft Production (from 1942) set an example in austerity.

Eden, Anthony (1897–1977)
Prime Minister from 1955 to 1957. Educated at Eton College and Oxford University, he became a Conservative M.P. in 1923. At 38 he became Foreign Secretary, but resigned over appeasement. He returned to that post under Churchill during the war and again in 1951. With Mr Attlee, he attended the San Francisco conference in 1945 to set up the United Nations Charter. He was knighted in 1954.

Edward VIII (1894–1972)
King for 11 months, January-December 1936. The son of King George V, he was trained as a naval cadet and studied at Magdalen College, Oxford. During World War One he joined the Grenadier Guards. A popular figure as Prince of Wales, he represented the King on tours at home and abroad. He was forced to abdicate owing to his wish to marry an American divorcee, and was later given the title Duke of Windsor.

Eisenhower, Dwight D. (1890–1970)
Soldier and President of the United States. Born in Texas, he went to West Point military academy, graduating in 1915. In 1942 he was sent to England to command U.S. forces in Europe and later that year became commander-in-chief of American and British forces invading North Africa. He commanded the Allied invasion of Europe in 1944. In 1952 and 1956 he was elected President of the United States.

▲ Winston Churchill inspects bomb damage in Battersea during the 1940 Blitz on London.

▲ George VI and Queen Elizabeth, their daughter Princess Elizabeth and her husband Prince Philip, and grandson Prince Charles.

Elizabeth II (1926–)
The eldest daughter of King George VI, she came to the throne on the death of her father in February 1952. As a girl she enjoyed country pursuits with horses and dogs, and spent the war years at Windsor. In 1945, on becoming eligible for National Service, she joined the A.T.S. as a driver and mechanic. In 1947 she married Lieutenant Philip Mountbatten, R.N., who was created Duke of Edinburgh.

Eliot, T. S. (1888–1965)
Poet and playwright. Born in St. Louis, Missouri, T. S. Eliot was educated at Harvard and Oxford. He settled in London in 1915 and became a naturalized British subject in 1927. His first book of verse was published in 1917. His well-known plays include *Murder in the Cathedral* (published in 1935) and *The Cocktail Party* (1949). He received a Nobel Prize in 1949.

Fleming, Alexander (1881–1955)
Educated at Kilmarnock Academy in Scotland and St. Mary's Hospital Medical School, Paddington, he was Professor of Bacteriology at London University from 1928 to 1948. In 1928 he discovered the first known antibiotic, penicillin, though it was several years before it could be manufactured as a practical drug. He was knighted in 1944 and received a Nobel Prize in 1945.

George VI (1895–1952)
The second son of King George V, he came to the throne when Edward VIII abdicated. He took on the task of restoring confidence in the monarchy and encouraged a distressed and weary nation during the difficult times of war. With the Queen (formerly Elizabeth Bowes-Lyon, whom he had married in 1923) he became deeply involved in Britain's progress towards peace and prosperity.

Hitler, Adolf (1889–1945)
The dictatorial ruler of Germany from 1933. Born in Austria, Hitler volunteered for the German Army during World War One. During the twenties he built up the strength of the Nazi Party, which dominated Germany from the early thirties. Hitler's vision of a German Third Reich demanded the subservience of all the German 'master race'. Having instigated policies of appalling barbarity, he killed himself.

Marshall, George C. (1880–1959)
American soldier and statesman. He served with the United States in France during World War One. In 1942 he travelled to London on behalf of President Roosevelt to propose aid to the Soviet Union and the launching of a second front. In 1947 he became Secretary of State. He promoted a plan for foreign aid, officially called the European Recovery Programme, known as the Marshall Plan.

Morrison, Herbert (1888–1965)
Labour politician and Cabinet minister. After leaving elementary school he worked as a telephone operator in a shop. In 1923 he was elected to Parliament, serving as Minister of Transport from 1929 to 1931. In the wartime coalition he was Home Secretary, giving his name to the 'Morrison' indoor air-raid shelter. During the post-war Labour government he was Deputy Prime Minister.

Mussolini, Benito (1883–1945)
Italian 'leader' and dictator. He founded the Fascist party in 1919, which promoted violent nationalism, and three years later was installed as Prime Minister. In 1925 he assumed dictatorial powers, suppressing all opposition. In 1940 Italy entered the Second World War on Germany's side, and when Italy was defeated by the Allies in 1943 Mussolini set up a Fascist government in northern Italy. He was killed by partisans in 1945.

Nuffield (Lord) (1877–1963)
Car manufacturer and philanthropist. Born William Morris, he was brought up in Oxford where at first he ran a cycle-repair business. His first car began production in 1912. He continued to run the Morris Motors firm until 1952, when it became part of the British Motor Corporation. He was made a baron in 1934. In addition to many charitable donations he founded Nuffield College, Oxford, and the Nuffield Foundation.

Orwell, George (1903–1950)
Journalist and author. Born in India, his real name was Eric Blair. During the Spanish Civil War he fought on the side of the Republicans: *Homage to Catalonia*, published in 1938, tells of his experiences. *Animal Farm* (1945) is a satire on revolution which becomes perverted by corrupt dictatorship, and *Nineteen Eighty-Four* is a disquieting projection published in 1949 of a Western world controlled by totalitarian power.

Stalin, Josef (1897–1953)
Leader of the Soviet Union from 1924 to 1953. Born in Georgia, he joined the Bolsheviks under Lenin. After a period of exile in Siberia he took part in the successful revolution of 1917. When Lenin died he defeated his rival Trotsky for control of the Communist Party and put into effect his plans to industrialize the Soviet Union. After the German invasion of 1941 he led the Soviet defence, rising to be Generalissimo.

Whittle, Frank (1907–)
Pioneer in the field of jet-propelled aircraft. Educated at Leamington College and Cranwell, he served as an officer in the R.A.F. After a two-year spell at Cambridge he was put on special duty attached to Power Jets Ltd. The first flights of jet-propelled aircraft with the Whittle engine were made in 1941. He was made a Fellow of the Royal Society in 1947 and was knighted in 1948. Jet-propelled aircraft are still used today.

▲ Vera Lynn entertained millions with her songs, and became known as the 'Forces' Sweetheart'.

Projects

Collecting Ephemera

▲ Everyday objects from the past, which were then considered to be of little value, are called 'ephemera'. Collecting ephemera from the period between 35 and 50 years ago can be a fascinating hobby. Some of your older relatives may have hoarded picture postcards from holidays, snapshots, souvenirs of great occasions or even ration books.

Cigarette cards were produced in series, showing film stars, railway engines, aircraft, sporting personalities and ships of the time. The Post Office issued commemorative stamps for special occasions such as the Festival of Britain or the coronations. Old gramophone records, comics, children's books, household ornaments and Utility goods still turn up at jumble sales.

If you have a camera you could build a photographic record of larger survivals. Look for an air-raid shelter being used as a garden shed, or an old cinema being used for bingo.

Reading list

Briggs, Susan, *Keep Smiling Through*, Weidenfeld & Nicolson, 1975.

Calder, Angus, *The People's War: Britain 1939-45*, Cape 1969, Panther 1971.

Cameron, James (ed), *Down Memory Lane: A Photo Album of Daily Life in Britain 1930-1953*, Dent 1980.

Harris, Nathaniel, *The Forties and Fifties*, Macdonald 1975.

Hoare, Robert, *World War Two*, Macdonald 1973.

Hopkins, Harry, *The New Look: A Social History of the Forties and Fifties in Britain*, Secker & Warburg 1963.

Hopkinson, Tom (ed), *Picture Post 1938-1950*, Penguin 1970.

Huggett, Frank E., *Goodnight Sweetheart: Songs and Memories of the Second World War*, W. H. Allen 1979.

Lane, Peter, *The Twentieth Century*, Batsford 1972.

Longmate, Norman, *How We Lived Then 1939-1953*, Hutchinson 1971, Arrow 1977.

Unstead, R. J., *The Thirties*, Macdonald 1974.

Unstead, R. J., *Incredible Century: A Pictorial History 1901-1970*, Macdonald 1974.

Songs We Used to Sing

◄ Before the outbreak of war, songs were either cheerfully or sentimentally romantic. Dance bands and their vocalists performed *Ida! Sweet as Apple Cider* or *Love Is The Sweetest Thing*. 'Honey' as an endearment entered the British vocabulary with the popularity of American songs, and the colour of a depressed mood was definitely blue from then on. People escaped from the blues with *The Clouds Will Soon Roll By* and *The Sunny Side Of The Street*.

The dangers and separations of wartime made popular such songs as *Wish Me Luck* (... as you wave me goodbye), *I'll Be Seeing You* (.. in all the old familiar places), *We'll Meet Again* (... don't know where, don't know when) and *Now Is The Hour* (... when we must say goodbye). This last one was a Maori song of farewell, the English version remembered by overseas Allies and G.I. brides sailing away.

Find the words of wartime songs and look for evidence of hope and courage. *There's A Boy Coming Home On Leave*, *The Homecoming Waltz* and *Home Sweet Home Again* show how important the simple word 'home' became to songwriters. The promise of an end to Blitz and blackout is seen in *When They Sound The Last All-Clear*, and *I'm Going To Get Lit Up* (... when the lights go up in London).

Community singing in factory canteens, army camps and air-raid shelters helped to keep morale high. Favourites were *Roll Out The Barrel*, *Bless 'Em All*, and *The Quartermaster's Stores*. One of the silliest went *Mairzy doats and dozy doats and liddle lamzey divey!*

Cover Your Hair for Safety

► As women started to work in factories, the slogan 'Cover Your Hair for Safety' became common. The most popular method was the headsquare turban, which is still used today:

1. Take a square piece of material, measuring between 50 cm and 70 cm. Make a triangle by folding it in half, corner to corner.

2. Place the folded edge (AB) at the back of your neck and lift the points A and B above your head, pulling the material close to the sides of your face. Hold these in one hand, and pull the points C under points A and B and let them rest on your forehead.

3. Tie points A and B together over the top of point C, then pull points C forward and tie the loose ends A and B beneath them. Tuck the ends and any stray hair inside the turban.

When material was in short supply, a square could be divided between two women along the line of the fold.

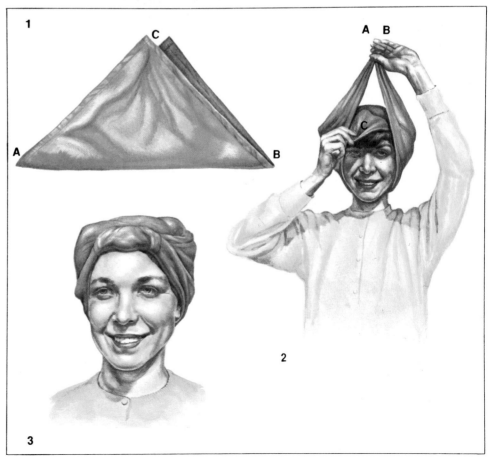

Index

PRINTED IN BELGIUM BY

proost
INTERNATIONAL BOOK PRODUCTION